HOW
Weather
THE STORM

My Guide to Overcoming Heartbreak, Connecting Back to Myself, and Thriving After Divorce

KAMEKA GRIFFIN

HOW TO Weather THE STORM

My Guide to Overcoming Heartbreak, Connecting Back to Myself, and Thriving After Divorce

KAMEKA GRIFFIN

Copyright © 2021 Kameka Griffin

Book by: Kameka Griffin
Printed in the United States of America
Publishing and Layout by: Crenterprise Consulting LLC
Edited by: Crenterprise Consulting LLC and Westbrook Media & Publishing
Cover Photo By: Travis A Malone
ISBN: 978-1-329-81909-2

Dedication

I want to dedicate my survival journey to my mom, Barbara Jean Alexander. I often think about the journey we had while I was growing up and how you gave birth to nine children. You didn't have much, but you loved us unconditionally and never stopped working to take care of us.

Your survival story is unmatched - from experiencing a brain aneurysm to surviving cancer! It was unexpected that at the age of 19, you would pass out in my arms from a brain aneurysm and how your strength would help me to tell my own story.

During my bad days, I remind myself that if my mom can survive a major vessel in her brain bursting, **I can survive this storm.** It looked uncertain to the doctors, family and friends and we thought God was calling you home. You beat the odds lady! Your brilliance always shined, through numerous doctor's appointments, multiple surgeries, and living in a nursing facility. Because you pressed through your challenges, I'm always empowered to see life differently.

Even in your sickness, you guided me. It's amazing that you can influence and lead someone without saying a mumbling word. That's how strong you are. You persevered through mama. For all of this, I say, thank you and I love you past eternity.

Foreword

As a Licensed, Master Level Social Worker for over 20 years and a close friend to Kameka, I offer a unique professional and personal perspective. I can say with full confidence that the author is for sure a great person to write this book on survival.

I met Kameka over 10 years ago and have watched her throughout a good part of her journey. I've witnessed her remain consistent while she kept Jesus as her source. Even on her hardest days, I witnessed her turn to God for strength and direction. She has a genuine heart that desires the best for all people with no expectation of a return on her investment - except to see others live their best life. She is a great mother who always displays her love and compassion toward her children, who are the centerpiece of her life.

As a professor, stylist, entrepreneur, and true woman of God on a mission, I have no doubt that this book will be written with a pure heart that seeks to assist others that find themselves on the same or a similar journey. It's sure to be a book that will change the hearts and minds of many due to its spiritual connection and sharing of such a powerful testimony by an even more powerful woman.

Tameika R. Crawford

Kameka Griffin, I have never been so thankful to know a person like you. Though we don't share the same bloodline, I have labeled you as my sister for life. You have inspired me in ways that you probably didn't realize. I will never forget when you first started doing my hair. I was heartbroken, stressed, and depressed. Then, after a few minutes of hearing me vent, you literally switched from my hair stylist to a counselor and lifted my spirits so high. We laughed, we cried, and you even shared some of your life experiences with me. You encouraged me to keep my head up, keep the faith, and to trust God in the process. You are the true epitome of what a strong black woman is and should be. So, in the words of the Golden Girls theme song "Thank you for being a friend, your heart is true, you're a pal and a confidant." I love you sis!

Nicole Brown

I have known Kameka Griffin for more than eleven years now. I heard about Kameka at a hair salon on American Way in Memphis, TN. The thing is, my beautician and Kameka worked in the same building. So, when I would get my hair done, Kameka was always in the back doing hair. I always heard her voice speak but had never seen her face. So, over the years it's been the same until my beautician decided to retire in 2010. And my beautician referred me to Kameka Griffin, the voice I always heard – but face I had never seen. This young lady has a glow and a smile, that would attract anyone to her heart. The strength I've seen Kameka have over the years can give anyone motivation regardless of what they may be going through. I always share personal information in my life with Kameka and she shares with me. She has an ear open to listen, gives advice, and is patience with people. The woman is very compassionate, loves her career, and is the only beautician I trust with my hair! I am glad to be a part of Kameka's life - not as a client, but as a friend.

Shannon Jones

When I think of my dearest friend Kameka, RESILIENT is the word that comes to mind. To see a woman, have someone to try and demean her and tear apart her character and to witness how she GRACEFULLY carried herself throughout the entire ordeal sets this woman apart from so many others. As a friend, I knew it was important to uplift and remind her that she is ENOUGH, and this too shall pass. I knew during that time, she needed someone to be there to pray for her strength and to ask God to keep her mentally.

I gained my sense of strength on behalf of the experience she dealt with. Because my sister/friend had already crossed that crossroad in her life, it allowed me lean on her when I was experiencing a difficult time during my marriage.

I love you girl, you're truly an inspiration!

Andrea Jones

Contents

Chapter 1

Disbelief of the Storm

"The most confused you will ever get is when you try to convince your heart and spirit of something your mind knows is a lie."

- **Shannon L. Alder**

I couldn't believe this was happening, and it felt like I was drowning in an out of body experience. It felt like I was in this deep lake. No, I'll use ocean to put it into perspective. During my travels overseas I used to always just think, "Oh my God, we are flying over this ocean and what if the plane fell in? How would we survive? Who would get us out of this water?" That was now me. Here I was trying to survive by constantly swimming to the top but was constantly pulled back into the abyss. I couldn't believe that I was drowning in this relationship.

Poker Face

The perception of drowning in a failed marriage wasn't a reality I was prepared for, and I would hide it at all costs. This led me to putting on a poker face like everything was ok.

So, why would I want to hide the turmoil of my marriage and sit in a state of mental disbelief? Well, I didn't want anybody to judge me. Besides, I had conquered something that a lot of people desire. What do I mean? A lot of women want to conquer marriage. A lot of women want to conquer having kids. A lot of women want to conquer buying a house and establish a middle-class foundation. Think about it. Together, you and your spouse generate six figures and serve as mentors to other people. When I read Facebook posts of us pictured together, I would receive comments like, "Power Couple" and "Black Love." Or friends and family would say things like "I want to be like you."

The consensus often expressed was that our family would be gathering, as usual, because we were the fun couple. We would host these big extravagant birthday parties and invite people to our home. Our house was the one that everybody came to and enjoyed themselves.

Other couples came to **us** for advice. People would literally come to me like, "Man, how did you do it?" How was I able to stay with somebody from high school and grow into adulthood together?

In all honesty, a core element of my disbelief was letting everyone else down and that feeling of failure was constant.

I thought that it was about other people until I began to realize that it's not. Let's use my wedding as an example. We sent out invitations to150 people and 200+ were in attendance. These were people that "loved and supported" us and wanted to see us happy, so I thought. I can recall going back to watch our wedding video and I honestly only remember a small portion because I was so concerned with our guests and making sure they were enjoying the wedding.

But, what about when you move out of that? I'm talking about when the wedding is done and the big spectacle has concluded, who is still there? When watching the wedding video, I realized that there were many people in attendance that I don't even talk to anymore. So, when you really reflect on the REALITY of it, you are paying for other people to come and see you get married.

I was putting on this poker face in front of people that I couldn't even call when my marriage went sideways. You don't know where they are, and they didn't have time to conversate when everything crashed. I couldn't call any of these people that I thought supported and loved me, because the reality is that they didn't care.

There is also the fact that a lot of people you think are praising you are really praying for your downfall. These days, I'm strategic about picking the people in my circle and you know I'm selective with people that come to my house.

New Marriage, New Storm

I was 27 when we got married and he was 25, and the signs of chaos were there early. Matter of fact, I felt the effects of a storm when purchasing our first home about a year after we got married.

At the time, we were going through a housing program and there were certain things you needed to have for eligibility. He checked the boxes on the things they wanted us to have with his income, credit, job tenure etc. That shouldn't have mattered because when you are married you should move as one, but it didn't feel that way.

I realized I was in a storm when the counselor that was assigned to us began to only direct conversations to him. I can remember this like it was yesterday. She didn't acknowledge me, and I felt that as my significant other, he should have recognized what she was doing and made the effort to make me feel comfortable with everything. Why couldn't he simply correct her in a professional way? Even when it was time to pick the house, he was like, "You don't even have what it takes to buy the house, so why would you have a say so in picking out the house?" All the while, I'm thinking, "You don't want my insight, but you still need my money to make it all work."

Also, I love to decorate homes, but my ideas were met on deaf ears. He gave off this aura of "I bought this house" and had the big head, so my decorative choices didn't matter.

This is so crazy because I found the company and did the research to bring the housing program to him. Picking a house is a woman's dream, and at this time I began to realize that I'm in a marriage where I don't even really have a say.

Everything I thought, read about, saw on TV shows, or observed from other couples about what a good life partner looked like didn't align with my situation.

I Still Stayed

Why would I stay in this storm? One reason is because I didn't know how to leave. We had just purchased the house and I was already feeling like I wasn't enough and couldn't make it happen on my own. How am I going to go and get another house?!At this point, I had been in my career since 18 and knew how to make money. Still, I wasn't the bread winner, IN MY HEAD. Then, there is the fact that I had two little children. I'm looking at these two little children, like, hey, they need their father. He may not be the best man, but he's a good father. He went to work every day and paid bills. I would ask myself, "Why are you going to leave and let another woman run in and take what you have?" And at the time, I thought the house we were staying in was a mansion. Why would I throw this away? Who is

When a child starts off with both parents, trying to build another foundation with another member would be difficult. Bringing someone into the picture who is not their biological parent is tough. Some women can just pick up the pieces and go on, but I can only speak for myself in stating that it's hard. When considering the future, I personally didn't want people around my kids, and don't mind doing a background check! You can go and get somebody else, but you can't replace the original mother and father.

Family Disbelief

Most people would think that family is supposed to be supportive, caring and on your side under these conditions – it's human nature. I won't say that they didn't, but it came off as "I don't want to be in that," and "that has nothing to do with me." They would often say, "Ya'll are going to get back together." They couldn't believe it and were in a state of shock as well because we had been together for so long. I recommend that you get a strong and understanding support system (friend or family) while fighting through a divorce because it's needed.

My family didn't know how deep it was because I held back, and this made it tougher because I don't share all my business. I would tell only what I wanted them to know. I didn't want to share what was happening because I wanted to look like this model couple. Having issues and problems wasn't the narrative I wanted out there. Surprisingly, I didn't want him to look bad in front of them. I did want them to know that he wasn't as nice as they thought he was.

I felt like my family was supposed to be calling me and texting me like, "Girl, don't worry about it!" "You want to go out to eat?" "You want to have a meltdown party?" No, I got none of that and felt pushed away because they felt like we would get back together. Yes, he had been in the family for 17 years, but I need you to be there for me!

I have a cousin that has taken his side 100%, and this isn't surprising because she doesn't like anybody in the family. In the beginning, I had a brother that sided with him until my ex started to show them something different.

On top of that, I really needed my family because after the downfall of my relationship, COVID happened. So, I had no choice, but to just sit in the house and dwell in my pain. The energy I did feel was, "We know you've been putting on," and there was a lack of compassion. This was a disbelief.

Notes

Chapter 2

Anger in the Storm

"Bitterness is like cancer. It eats upon the host. But anger is like fire. It burns it all clean."

-   **Maya Angelou**

What made me the angriest in this relationship? I can recall an incident with my niece who is the same age as our daughter. A situation occurred that resulted in her being homeless. And when I say homeless, I'm not talking about going from house to house. She was living on the street with her mother. I wouldn't let this happen to my brother's daughter, so she moved in with us. One day, I overheard him talking about the situation and about me to his friend over the intercom. I became so angry with him because I'm thinking, "Hey, that's our niece." She's been coming around us forever and it shouldn't have been a big problem with her moving in temporarily when we have the space. Now, I understood, in a sense, why he was upset because I didn't initially come to him before making the decision. My thoughts were, "Surely, he would have a heart for this child because she's living on the street." He didn't have to do anything financially for her, and she just needed a bed. Nevertheless, we had different views on, and I couldn't believe that I married somebody with this type of heart. This caused me to become angry with myself for choosing such a partner.

There was another incident that involved my mother being in the hospital. It was a severe situation, and we didn't know what the outcome was going to be. My family would rotate shifts at the medical facility to make sure someone was always there with my mother. It was my turn to sit with my mom, and I had a time conflict because my daughter had and this was confirmed when I saw this same cheap lotion for sale in Walgreens! This was a trigger for me.

I was triggered when taking my daughter to her dance coach's house because of the area she lived in. It's sad to say that her dance coach stayed in the same vicinity where I caught him cheating. To deal with this particular trigger, I would go out my way and take the long route to her coach's house just to avoid the area where his infidelity took place.

Many of my friends would cause triggers that made me angry. One of my friends had an issue with the law, and because she knew his occupation was in law enforcement, she called me asking for his number. During our conversation, she said his name. At the time, even his name was a trigger for me! So, I let her finish everything that she had to tell me and at the end of our conversation I told her that she can't call me asking anything about him because that's a trigger for me.

On an off day, I went to work to get my son's hair cut and a conversation sparked between my coworker and myself. I was just telling him how excited I am to be writing this book but didn't give him full detail because I wanted to surprise people. I've also learned that you can't always share your good intentions with people because they may give off negativity. Nevertheless, he asked what it was about, and I told him "relationships." That opened the conversation about my relationship, and he wanted to know if I had talked to my ex. Ultimately, his assessment was, "You aren't over it." So, I had to give him a whole story about it and let him know that he could not tell me when to be over it. We began to discuss how his brother had just passed 3 years ago. I empathetically asked, "Are you over it?" His answer was

"No" and once I explained it from that angle, he was like, "You know what…. You're so right." I couldn't tell him when to get past the death of his brother and he had no right to tell me that I wasn't over it. A time limit can't be placed on how long it takes for someone to heal or get over trauma.

I've had to face triggers when it came to my children's activities. Of course, when you are in a marriage, both parents are tied to communications about your kid's extracurricular activities – such as group chat. In the coaches group chat, I still had to see his name come up and this was a trigger. Because I didn't want to see his name, I deleted it from my phone, but then the number popped up. Well, I didn't like the phone number coming up either! I decided to put "Nobody" as his title to deal with the trigger.

I've experienced triggers with my daughter and my son being at the house where he cheated. I was following my daughter on TikTok and watching her have fun, as she deserves. However, the background in her dance video was at *that* house. This was a trigger and I decided to stop following my daughter on TikTok.

A colossal trigger occurred this year in February. It was snowing bad outside, and he said he couldn't drive in the snow because he didn't have a vehicle that wouldn't get stuck. He suggested that I come and pick them up. Having to come to *that* house and pick up my kids was crushing.

This journey has taught me that you don't know what true triggers are until you have walked in these shoes. And it's okay to deal with those triggers on your terms.

I Feel Sorry for Her

What I feel is not even so much anger towards her because she is a non-factor, even though, she's in the position of being called all the names that I could think of. I almost feel sorry for her. She's like a child that knows not what she has done. I don't care how good it may look or feel, you never should have been with a married man. Just know that you will have your day. It's a serious thing to interfere with marriage regardless of what he may have told her. Karma is very real, and it will come for you. What she has done and the role that she played must be atoned for by destiny.

Anger Got Me Arrested

One day, I went over to his new house to get my kids and now that I think about it, this was an out-of-body experience. Trust me when I say that you are not yourself when you snap. Now, I understand, that nobody can judge because you don't know what you would do if you snapped. And when it comes to your children, it will fuel that anger.

So, on that day, I was feeling angry and hurt and had turned into to somebody that wasn't me. So, instead of knocking on the door or announcing my presence, I parked my car fast, got out and I went through his open garage and made my way to the doorway. He didn't see me pull up, and it startled him, but he still managed to block the doorway to keep me from getting in. In the moment, he was standing in the doorway already on the phone with the police.

The police called him because I had just left the precinct reporting how he wouldn't give me my kids! I went there like, "Hey, y'all, he won't give me my kids! Here's my paperwork. Here is where it says that I am supposed to get my kids back!" They said that they would call him and talk to him and that they couldn't just snatch my kids from him. They took too long to follow up and it may have been 5 minutes, but it felt like 5 hours, and this made me angry.

Let's get back to the encounter. I walked through the garage and made it to the door, and he tried to close it on me. He began screaming like I was trying to rob him or something! I was prepared to push my 125 pounds against this police officer into this house to get to my kids. I could tell that I frightened him, and he just released his hands off the door, and I made my way in.

Once I got in the house, I didn't touch anything and just started screaming my kid's names, "Kelsei, Kameron, y'all come on, I'm here to get you!!" He started screaming at me to get out and his partner came around the corner. I looked at her and said, "Oh, Hey girl. I'm just here to get my kids." She didn't curse me out or tell me to get out of her house. At that moment, she couldn't do anything but feel me because these were MY kids! But of course, this was her man, and he told her to get the camera to start recording me. So, my response was, "Oh, it's fine. I said I'm just here to get my kids!" Kelsei came down the stairs and she was trying to get to me, but he kept jumping in the middle. Kelsei then threw me her purse and I grabbed it and finally left out the house when my daughter started to cry.

I could have easily driven away from their property but didn't touch anything, so I just sat there until my sisters drove up. My sisters waited on the police with me, and when they arrived, the drama unfolded even more.

He told the police I kicked the door in and embellished the story instead of just telling them that I had come over to get my kids. His statement led to them telling me to "turn around" as they were going to put those handcuffs on me. I looked up and saw him standing in the garage, with her, in the presence of my kids and I began to feel so weak. The feeling can be likened to a snail that shrinks when salt is applied. I felt so small like the worst person in the world. "Oh my God, what will my kids think about me now?"

At that moment, I realized that he didn't even see me as his children's mother anymore.

Well, they threw it out and I didn't get locked up, but that was enough for me, and I learned something. It's important that you understand the law and consider the bigger picture even when you are angry. Let's say that the children are at the father's house, and it is time to bring them back home. Even if you have made a notarized agreement with the other parent, I was advised that it is not legal documentation if the judge has not signed off on it.

If you experience a situation like mine, I advise you to first, stop and breathe. Get a hold of yourself. Ask yourself if it's even worth what you are about to do. Call the police and have them go over there with you. The police still cannot take your kids, but they can do a report on it. If your child is not in any danger, just wait and get the children back the next day. Everything doesn't require your energy and for you to become mentally disturbed.

If you must cry, go cry out in the car, cry it out at home or cry to somebody. Understand that you are really fighting off emotions, hurt, pain, and those little thoughts in your head.

It's ok to talk to someone about the situation who can give great advice. When I was just talking to the wrong people, they would just advise me to react, and they had never walked in my shoes. You want to talk to somebody positive who has experience on what you're going through. You need that somebody who will say, "Girl, calm down. Your children are ok. I know you're ready for them to come back home but know that they are with their father who isn't going to do anything to them." "Girl, If he wanted more time with his kids, allow him more time with his kids." A true friend would share that he's not taking any love from you because they are with him.

Coping with Anger

Handling anger required me to recognize the triggers and create strategies to overcome them. Like, if kids are supposed to be back at eight, but I receive a phone call that he is going to bring them back at nine, I'll tell myself, "Okay, it's only one more hour." So, I would go and walk in the park. I would read. I might go and get my nails done. I might listen to some music. I might clean up. I would do positive things to pass the time and not let negative thoughts fester into anger.

In the past, I didn't like a lot of noise, but now I like it because it was a coping mechanism. Sometimes, I come in the house and turn up my music sky high. Why? You need some noise going instead of just sitting idle in the silence.

I had to realize that I didn't even want him to win by me being angry. If I continued to be angry, it would make him happy. That was motivation to get my mind together and coach myself out of that mental state. This revelation made me want to approach things a different way, you know.

Social Media

Social media contributed to the anger I felt. During the relationship, we always posted pictures and shouted each other out. There would be times when we could have just had a huge fight, but I would keep the social media show going by posting his picture. The last anniversary trip we went on was two months before we broke up, and I had a meltdown with him because he didn't want to go. No one would have known that he didn't want to go on that anniversary trip because I posted pictures on social media showing us in a happy state. I wanted to continue looking like this "Cosby Couple" to the world. My grandmother's nephew would always post under our pictures that we were "Beyonce and Jay Z." We looked good to everyone for so long and breaking the image that I worked hard to build made me angry.

I never wanted to be that couple that beefed on social media. I used social media to tell my truth, advertise my business, and share happy moments. However, social media became the worst because it was showing me in a negative way. I felt that everyone was in my business and my full life was on display for the world to judge. People that I knew and didn't know had access to my life and it became overwhelming. I learned to move differently when posting things because I didn't want to feed more into the circus.

Accusations were made against me on social media that were so untrue. One accusation involved me cursing my kids out for wanting to spend time with their father (so untrue)! So many people started commenting and attacked my character! They even advised him to take me to court and take my kids away. Nevertheless, I didn't retaliate and stayed silent.

Notes

Chapter 3

Accepting the Storm

"You've got to learn to leave the table when love's no longer being served."

- Nina Simone

I quit! For most of our lives, we are taught that quitting is for losers. "Winners never quit, and quitters never win." I discovered while this is not inaccurate, it is incomplete. There are times in life when we must decide to quit to win. I quit being unhappy! I quit settling for less than what I deserved! I quit putting up with my history, forfeiting my destiny! I had to grapple with the fact that my marriage was completely over. I accepted my storm.

My storm came with so many questions: What's Next? What do I do after being with the same person for 17 years of my life? What do I do about housing arrangements? What do I do about money? Will I love again? Who am I mad at? Is this my fault? Who do I turn to? Who do I listen to? Do I fight for the house? Do I fight for alimony? What do I do about insurance? What are my rights? Even with all these unanswered questions, I accepted this violent disturbance that came to knock the wind, the very life out of me called divorce.

I had to learn to let go. Letting go included letting go of all the materialistic items we accumulated together. Often, we try to avoid our storms because we want to hold on to a house, a car, memories, and our place of comfort. To make it to the other side of a storm, you've got to be willing to leave some things behind.

Keep Moving

By accepting my storm, I permitted myself to move on. I refused to allow this divorce to take me out. I learned my rights and wasn't going out without a fight. Can you imagine the one you once loved and vowed to share a "til death do us part" kind of love with stop paying the mortgage? Can you imagine the father of your children divorcing his duties to care for his seeds? I was left to take care of my children by myself. That was not enough to stop me. I wanted to make sure my children could enjoy life as they had always known it. I made a promise to myself that they would not be casualties of my storm. The truth of the matter is this was not a storm to them; they were relieved. They were exhausted from all the bickering, yelling they were forced to witness in my unhealthy marriage.

Storms come with rain, thunderstorms, and you better believe that I was experiencing a complete uproar. Not only was I going through a divorce, but I also had to close my business and deal with an ill-equipped attorney. People say that experience is the best teacher. It doesn't have to be your very own experience.

Find A Good Attorney

If you're going through a divorce, make sure you do intensive research to ensure you have someone advocating for you who is knowledgeable. I did not! This caused me to lose victories in court that belonged to me. As if my divorce from my husband wasn't enough, my attorney was trying to divorce me at the same time. She decided that she no longer wanted to practice family law and thought it would be a

Chapter 4

Finding Peace in the Storm

"Peace cannot be kept by force. It can only be achieved by understanding."

- Albert Einstein

I thought I was weak because I was receiving shots and not returning them. I was being talked about, lied on, my name was being scandalized, I became a target for foolishness, and I chose not to fire back when I had plenty of ammunition. When I got to the place, I was no longer angry or revengeful is the place where I found sweet peace. I chose calmness over anxiety. I chose boundaries over drama. I decided to tame my tongue and not be triggered. I could've engaged in the tug of war but decided that recess was for the immature and miserable. I set out to protect the peace that I had finally found.

My peace was personal. Initially, I needed people around me to walk me through the storm. The truth is, when you're going through, you don't need too many voices. It was author Sarah Louisgnau who wrote, "You can't find happiness with an outside-in approach, it has to originate within you. When you master your inner thoughts, you can feel like an ordinary everyday superhero."

I had to limit my conversations with those I love to protect my peace. Many people who had a heart to help me were hurting me. They didn't know what to say, what not to say, or how to be calm amid my storms. Peace meant that I could not be silent about my feelings. I found myself in a season where I had to teach people how to treat me. When people have not walked in your shoes in your storm, they don't understand. Comprehension wasn't a requirement; respect was.

I Cried Out to God

It was through this, the most frustrating time in my life, that I found peace. I remember crying out to God regularly. Crying doesn't make us weak; it makes us human. It's alright to cry, especially when we have a God to cry to. When we cry out to our heavenly father, He hears us. It was significant for me to allow myself to feel what I felt whether it was sadness, loneliness, or grief. When you're trying to find peace while coping with pain, own your feelings. Acknowledge the pain to heal.

Healing Is For You

The dynamic between myself and his family was also a challenge. Some of them wanted to stay connected. I tried, but it felt so strange. I felt weird and out of place discussing their family member. Some of them were even clients. I wanted to continue to do their hair and talk to them, but things they would say were triggers for me. They would share how they saw him living his "new life" and how they really didn't like it. I didn't want to hear any of that. I felt like they were lying. Or maybe they wanted to say something to make me feel good or feel that they really cared about me. Ultimately, he was still their family, and I couldn't be mad about that.

You cannot heal trying stay connected to something that has wounded you. If you're trying to heal a little sore on your arm but constantly keep hitting it against the dresser, it won't heal. You need to find another route in the room to get around that dresser. That dresser will stand whether you hit it or not, but what are you going to do? What I'm saying is that the healing is for you, not them. They won't understand it, but they got to respect it. I made the decision to break those relationships once I realized that healing wasn't for them, but it was for me.

Healing is a process that doesn't happen overnight. It takes peace to progress to healing. After healing, then comes forgiveness. In the spirit of transparency, I have not fully forgiven my ex-husband. I know that forgiveness is for me and not him. I know that unforgiveness is equivalent to drinking poison daily and expecting the other person to die. I get it. Yet, I am not there. It's a process, and I own my truth while striving for better. I have mastered peace, but I am still trying to get there as it relates to forgiveness.

I must admit that before my storm, I knew God, but I didn't "know" God. I've been robbed before and recognized that man couldn't have possibly saved me. I was positive that there was a higher power. However, the supernatural peace I found in my storm could only be poured out by an almighty God. I intensified my prayer life. As a result, when I thought I was losing it, I indeed found Him.

I was in a bad season while enjoying a new relationship with peace. My mindset was changing; my perspectives were shifting. God used me to motivate others, to lift them while I was supposed to be down myself. People tried to pick me apart, but peace spoke up for me.

Where Is Peace

Someone once asked me, where do I find peace? What do I do for peace? I am at the peak of my peace when having family night with my children. We laugh, we love, and we live a beautiful life together. I admit I had to throw every piece of furniture away that my ex and I purchased together. It had to go so peace could stay.

I discovered that peace isn't the absence of problems. Peace means that your problems will not have control over you. I became my children's primary guardian, which means I became the sole disciplinarian. I had to not only fight in the divorce, but I had to fight to make sure that my children understood I was not the enemy.

My ex no longer had the responsibility of parenting them daily. He no longer had to look at the bigger picture. I was left to be the "no" parent. The parent who says no is often the one who appears to be strict and unreasonable. Honestly, my children are blessed to have a father who loves them, although our parenting styles are different. I refuse to be the "yes" parent. I am committed to taking care of my children and raising them in the way they should go. My children don't always love my response to their every desire, but they don't question my love.

For anyone reading this and trying to find peace in a storm, I encourage you to pray. We often use prayer like a fire extinguisher; we only use it when the fire breaks out. If the only time we are praying is when we are in trouble, we are already in trouble. Prayer should be just as natural, consistent as breathing, just like we breathe to live. We should pray to have peace.

When you pray, rest assure that you can flip the page and enter a new chapter. So many believe that a spouse is to complete them. I challenge that thought. When we marry, we should already be complete, and gaining a spouse should only compliment who we already are. You did not die. You got a divorce. There is still life in you. There is still value in you. Allow God to show you what's next.

Notes

Chapter 5

New Beginnings After the Storm

"No storm can last forever. It will never rain 365 days consecutively. Keep in mind that trouble comes to pass, not to stay."

- Iyanla Vanzant

There is a song that says, "My rearview can't compare to what God will do in my life." Our past is familiar, and we tend to replay it repeatedly. What could I have done differently? How could they have done that to me? Why did I stay so long? We cannot spend too much time looking at what's behind us. If we're driving a car and looking backward, we're going to crash. That said, it's unhealthy to stay in a storm when we have the power to overcome it.

Many times, we try to nurse our hurt. Have you ever seen someone who went to the hospital for something minor but kept their hospital band on their wrist for several days? Truthfully, we want people to know that we've been wounded. Being wounded gets us attention when what we should be seeking is healing. I was not going to become stagnant in my storm. After the chaos is when I began to breathe again so I could move on.

Parenting After the Storm

Moving on means facing my new reality. My children now have two parents, living in separate homes and with two standards of living. I never wanted my children to have stepparents. I surely never wanted them to be introduced to someone who would be in a relationship with my ex while we were very much so still married. How can someone who has disrespected me love my children? Is that even possible? Nevertheless, this was the hand that I was dealt. I wouldn't say I liked it. The fact of the matter is I had to get over it.

Let's be honest after the storm means that I won't always be single. My "after the storm friend" showers me with gifts and has even proposed. When you come through a storm as I endured, you don't enter marriage lightly. You don't enter anything quickly. As of now, I am not ready. Yes, I am dating. Yes, I am rebuilding. Not only do I have to protect myself, but I also have a more significant duty to protect my children. Protecting them means waiting it out, taking my time, unlike their father did. Yes, I threw a little shade, but it's my book about my storm, and I have the authority to tell it how I feel it.

Seriously, protecting my children doesn't include keeping them away from their father. The goals for co-parenting should have the best interest of the children at heart. I once read an article entitled, *Co-Parenting and Joint Custody Tips for Divorced Parents* that I'd like to share a few:

1. **Set hurt and anger aside-** Successful co-parenting means that your own emotions—any anger, resentment, or hurt—must take a back seat to the needs of your children.

2. **Strive to communicate effectively-** Peaceful, consistent, and purposeful communication with your ex is essential to the success of co-parenting—even though it may seem impossible.

3. **Try to Co-parent as a team-** Parenting is full of decisions you'll have to make with your ex, whether you like each other or not. Cooperating and communicating without blow-ups or bickering makes decision-making far easier on everybody.

4. **Make transitions and visitation easy-** The actual move from one household to another, whether it happens every few days or just certain weekends, can be a challenging time for children. Every reunion with one parent is also a separation with the other; each "hello" is also a "goodbye."

Admittedly, I must pray and release them. Even after he unsuccessfully attempted to take my children from me, I did not retaliate. I desire that my children be loved, feel loved by their mother and father. After all, we divorced each other, but that doesn't mean we divorced them.

After the storm, I am adjusting to my new normal. Not having my children in my house for two weeks during the Christmas season is part of my after-the-storm experience. I check in with them, but I allow their time with their dad to be just that. I want them to enjoy their time together, but if I'm honest, it is an adjustment.

After the storm is literally like being in the recovery room after having surgery. The surgery is over, and now it's time to heal. There are fresh wounds that need your attention. The healing process can be a place of discomfort. Embrace the journey. Make the necessary adjustments. Develop healthy coping strategies. I listen to motivational

Key Takeaways

_____

_____

_____

_____

_____

_____

_____

_____

_____

_____

_____

_____

Key Takeaways

Key Takeaways

Key Takeaways

_____

_____

_____

_____

_____

_____

_____

_____

_____

_____

_____

_____

Key Takeaways

Acknowledgements

There was one time when I cried out to my cousin, Krystal Bridgefort and told her, "I'm about to check into Lakeside" because mentally, I had just about had it. She said, "No!" She told me to dry my tears, get on top of it, and write the book that I talked about. That day, I started writing, and it felt weird, but I did it. So, thank you cousin for always being there.

I want to acknowledge Kristy Wilson who doesn't even know how she inspired me to write a book when she came into my shop. She is a great author, and I mentioned my interest in writing a book and she started sending me all types of information to get started, but I never made a move – until now! So, thank you for that initial push and inspiration to show me that it is possible.

One day I sent my sister Felecia a message that I'm bruised and **broken**. She said, "No, you may be a little bruised, but you are definitely not broken!" She reminded me of the great things that I have done and that she saw the future in me, and I thank her for that.

My sister April went through a similar storm and was in a dark place like me. It had gotten so bad that she didn't want to get up in the morning and didn't even want to comb her hair. She is like a light bulb now and has inspired me to get up and go! When you see her now, she is glamourous all the time and full of life! She experienced her storm while I was still married. I recall saying what she should be doing but now realize that I shouldn't have been putting my mouth on her situation. I didn't truly understand then, but I do now.

God rebirth her and she also gave birth to a new baby. Thank you, sister, for being the inspiration I needed.

As I watched my sister Jennifer Baker become a new wife, execute wifely duties, adopt a child, raise that child, and stay in connection with the child's mother, it is a true encouragement. It drives me to stay connected to my children and stay motivated.

My late brother Eugene Harris was an inspiration to me. He was 47 when he passed and put up a great fight against diabetes and challenges of life. He had never had his own place but got to the point in the final stages of his life where he got his own place and was in a happy place.

If you need a listening ear to hear you go off and vent, that would be my brother Contrell!

My brother Marlon always tells me that, "You are beautiful! You better go and get you somebody else!" That positive affirmation and love is very much appreciated.

My older sister Rosalyn would tell me, "You are doing it! You are doing good!" Rosalyn has successfully fought through her storms of life from having cancer, to having a taking care of her daughter who got sick and much more. I admire your strength and appreciate you.

Thank you to my little sister Melody who exhibits true perseverance as she pursues her passion of dance. I love you and encourage you to keep going!

Most importantly, I want to thank God for allowing me to be broken down so that I could be built back up. I lost my house, my car was hit and taken away, and everything seemed to be leaving. He restored everything and rebuilt my mental in a way that no counselor could ever do. When I couldn't call on anybody, God never left my side. I encourage anyone who is going through a traumatic experience to understand that you WILL NOT be able to do it without God. He showed me his true power and I give him all the glory and praise. Thank you, God, for showing me my true path, and I owe it all to you.

About the Author

Kameka Griffin is a successful Hairstylist, Licensed Salon Owner and Cosmetology Instructor from Memphis, TN.

Kameka grew up in the historic community of Orange Mound with 9 siblings and graduated from the Melrose High School.

Kameka resides in Olive Branch, MS and is the proud mother of her daughter, Kelsei Temple, and her son Kameron Temple.